With much thanks to Sue Whitney

WE BOTH READ®

Parent's Introduction

We Both Read is the first series of books designed to invite parents and children to share the reading of a story by taking turns reading aloud. This "shared reading" innovation, which was developed in conjunction with early reading specialists, invites parents to read the more sophisticated text on the left-hand pages, while children are encouraged to read the right-hand pages, which have been written at one of three early reading levels.

Reading aloud is one of the most important activities parents can share with their child to assist their reading development. However, *We Both Read* goes beyond reading *to* a child and allows parents to share reading *with* a child. *We Both Read* is so powerful and effective because it combines two key elements in learning: "showing" (the parent reads) and "doing" (the child reads). The result is not only faster reading development for the child, but a much more enjoyable and enriching experience for both!

Most of the words used in the child's text should be familiar to them. Others can easily be sounded out. You may find it helpful to read the entire book aloud yourself the first time, then invite your child to participate on the second reading. Also note that the parent's text is preceded by a "talking parent" icon: ☺ ; and the child's text is preceded by a "talking child" icon: ☺ .

We Both Read books is a fun, easy way to encourage and help your child to read—and a wonderful way to start your child off on a lifetime of reading enjoyment!

We Both Read: My Day

––––––––––––––––––––––

We Both Read® is a trademark of Treasure Bay, Inc.

Published by Treasure Bay, Inc.
40 Sir Francis Drake Blvd.
San Anselmo, CA 94960 USA

PRINTED IN SINGAPORE

Library of Congress Catalog Card Number: 2002 103856

Hardcover ISBN: 1-891327-43-7
Paperback ISBN: 1-891327-44-5

05 06 07 08 09 / 10 9 8 7 6 5 4 3

We Both Read® Books
Patent No. 5,957,693

Visit us online at:
www.webothread.com

My Day

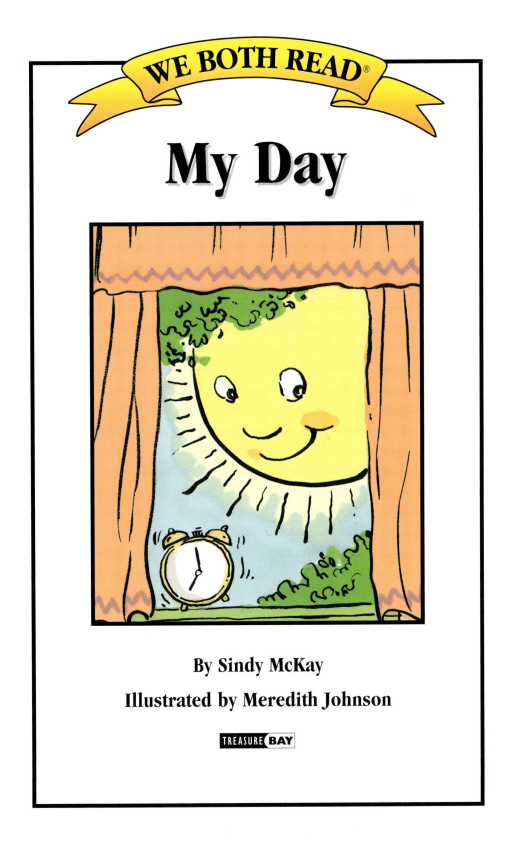

By Sindy McKay

Illustrated by Meredith Johnson

TREASURE BAY

I hear my clock ringing. My day has begun.

My day always starts with my good friend the . . .

. . . sun.

My mom says, "It's time to get up, sleepy head!
It's time to get up and get out of your . . .

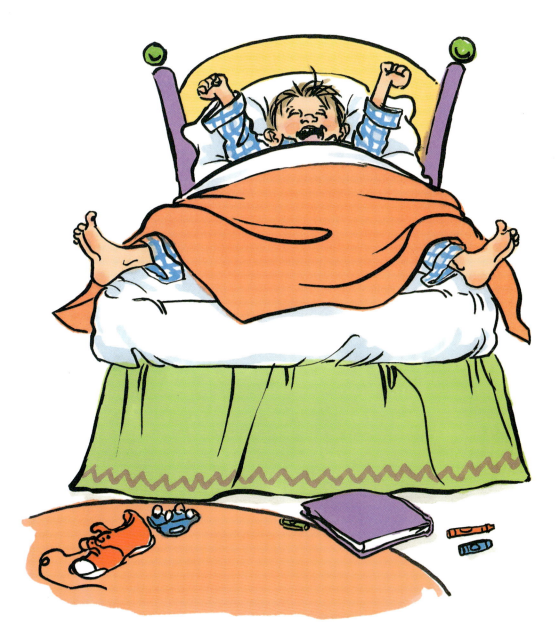

. . . bed."

I rush to get dressed. I know just what to choose!
I find both my socks. Then I look for my . . .

. . . shoes.

It's time to wash up—make the dirt disappear!

I take extra care when I clean out my . . .

. . . ear.

I run down the hall with my doggie named Tom.

We rush to the kitchen and both hug . . .

. . . my mom.

My mom gives me toast with the butter-side up.

She gives me some juice in my favorite blue . . .

 . . . cup.

Old Tom likes toast, too. (He's a bit of a hog.)

But Mom gives him food that is made for . . .

. . . a dog.

My mom says to hurry—there's no time to fuss!

I race down the sidewalk and hop on . . .

. . . the bus.

We head off for school—we don't want to be late!
Our teacher is waiting for us by the . . .

. . . gate.

She leads us inside and we sit on a rug.

She reads us a story about a . . .

. . . big bug.

We draw and we cut and we use lots of glue.

And when we use crayons, I always choose . . .

. . . blue.

At lunch I sit next to my friend Patrick Napes.

He loves to eat apples, but I prefer . . .

. . . grapes.

It's back to the classroom to learn this and that.

We learn about numbers and how to spell . . .

Cat

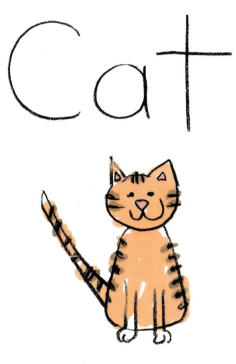

 . . . cat.

The final bell rings. It's too loud to ignore!
I jump up from my desk and I rush out . . .

. . . the door.

The bus picks me up. We drive right by a lake!

At home waiting for me is milk and some . . .

. . . cake.

I play with my toys and watch TV a tad.

I hear a car coming! I know it's . . .

. . . my dad.

We're hungry for dinner. We help as we're able.

My dad carries food out, and I set the . . .

. . . table.

It's time for my bath. Here I go! Rub-a-dub!

Dad turns on the water and fills up . . .

. . . the tub.

The sun has gone down now. Mom peeks in to look.

I'm ready for bed—after we read . . .

. . . a book.

Mom tucks me in tight and I'll be asleep soon.

My day always ends with my good friend . . .

. . . the moon.

If you liked *My Day*, here are two other *We Both Read*® Books you are sure to enjoy!

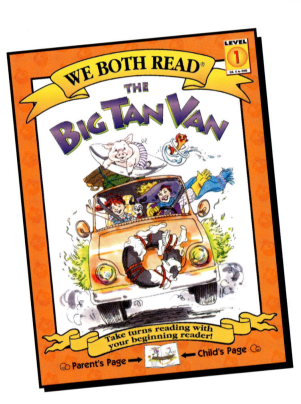

A wild ride of imagination awaits every reader of this Level 1 story for beginning readers. Aunt Sue takes her niece on a ride of adventure that brings them to some places you can only find in a book! There's a store with clothes that have cats and pans in the pockets, a park with jogging frogs, and a zoo that is run by the animals!

To see all the We Both Read books that are available,
just go online to **www.webothread.com**

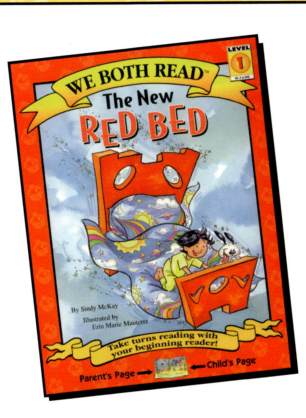

A very whimsical tale of a boy and his dog and their fantastic dreamland adventures. This delightful tale features fun and easy to read text for the beginning reader, such as "pigs that dig", "fish on a dish", and a "dog on a frog."